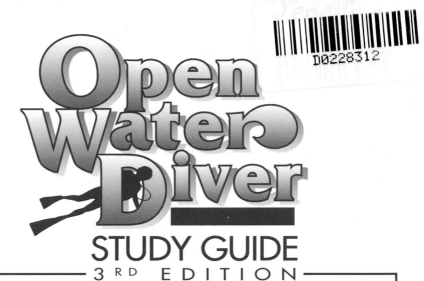

Open Water Diver

STUDY GUIDE

3RD EDITION

© Copyright 1995, 1992, 1990 by Concept Systems, Inc.

ISBN: 1-880229-30-7

First Edition
    First Printing, 1/90
    Second Printing, 9/90
Second Edition
    First Printing, 10/92
Third Edition
    First Printing, 12/95

Printed in the USA.

SCUBA SCHOOLS INTERNATIONAL

2619 Canton Court • Fort Collins, CO 80525-4498
(970) 482-0883 • Fax (970) 482-6157

Contents

REORDER # 2202

INTRODUCTION

This study guide reintroduces some of the main points covered in the manual and videos. It is designed as a memory aid. You will recall things you read in the book and fill in the blanks. It is important for you to realize that the study guide is not so much a *test of your knowledge* as an *assistant to your learning*. Therefore, it might benefit you more to fill in the answers as well as you can from memory, rather than by following along with the manual.

The best way to use this study guide and not cheat yourself is to read a chapter of the manual, view the video, and then quiz yourself by doing the corresponding section of the study guide. You might use a pencil so that you can go back and change incorrect answers. The study guide is not an exam for your instructor to grade; it is a tool to aid your personal understanding of the concepts and skills of the course.

We recommend you do the study guide from memory first, and *then* refer back to the manual to fill in blanks and correct wrong answers. The workbook will probably be more valuable to you if used this way.

Making use of your study guide can be a fun part of your course, but it can also give you a useful gauge of your progress, and will certainly help prepare you for your written exam.

C A U T I O N : *This educational system is not designed as an entire scuba course. While the academic requirements can be met wholly or partly through home study, it is nevertheless required that you complete pool and open water instruction under the direction of an SSI-certified instructor.*

Good luck, and good diving!

CHAPTER 1 STUDY QUESTIONS

1. The word *scuba* stands for _Self-contained Underwater breathing Apparatus._

2. Diving's foundation is equipment; that's why it is referred to as an _equipment-intensive_ sport.

3. There are two basic types of masks: the _low volume_ and the _high volume_.

4. _nose pockets_ built into masks are used for equalizing pressure inside the ears and sinuses.

5. The objective in finding a mask that fits is to match the _mask skirt_ and your _face_.

6. Fins come in two basic styles: the _full foot_ and the _open heal_.

7. With _open heal_ fins, adjust the strap to keep the booted foot firmly in place.

8. Some snorkels are equipped with a _self draning purge_ valve below the mouthpiece .

9. Water absorbs body heat _25_ times faster than air.

10. _Dive skins_ become more popular each year as technology improves the quality of the fabrics available.

11. Most recreational diving is done in temperatures between about 50°F (10°C) and 80°F (27°C). Coverage and thickness preferences come into play at the warm and cold extremes of this range, but it is generally agreed that full wet suits should be worn from _65°F to 75°F_.

12. Having a suit which conforms to your body cuts down on sags and gaps, assuring less water exchange and therefore less _heat loss_, and greater _comfort_.

13. You may want to consider using a _dry suit_ in waters below 60°F (16°C).

14. Most exposure suits "float," making the diver's body _positively_ _buoyant_.

15. The weight belt counteracts that _added_ _buoyancy_ and also helps the diver whose body is _natural_ _bouyant_, regardless of added buoyancy, to get below the surface.

16. The ability to see, breathe, and move are necessary elements of snorkeling, but to enhance the efficiency and comfort of these elements, the diver's buoyancy needs to be controlled by a _buoyance_ _compresen_.

17. _Weight_ _belt_ _ditching_ is a very important skill, and you and your buddy need to know how to remove your own as well as each other's _belt_ quickly and in the same way every time.

18. The snorkel is positioned on the _left_ side of the head and is attached to the mask strap by a _snorkle_ _keeper_.

19. Because you become slightly less coordinated when wearing the fins on dry land, they are generally the _last_ thing you put on.

20. When using any method other than the controlled seated entry, grip your _mask_ and _weight_ _belt_ firmly to keep them in place during entry.

21. Clear the snorkel by blowing a quick, sharp blast of air through it; this is called the _popping_ _method_.

22. The _flutter_ kick is the most basic and most often used.

23. The method for orally inflating a BC at the surface is called _bobbing_.

24. In snorkeling, you and your buddy should follow the _one up_, _one down_ system. While one of you dives, the other stays on the surface.

25. After using the suit, rinse each piece in _clean_, _fresh_ _water_.

CHAPTER 2 STUDY QUESTIONS

1. BCs are deflated in one of two ways. The air can be released slowly by pushing the ___manual___ ___control___ ___buton___ on the inflator mechanism, or it can be released quickly through a ___dump valve___ .

2. A safety feature built into BCs is the ___overexpansion___ ___relief___ valve which is designed to let air bleed off when the BC overexpands.

3. The tank is the foundation of the sport of scuba diving. Combined with the regulator it forms a ___self___ – ___contained___ ___air supply___ which enables the diver to remain under water untethered.

4. When choosing a tank, realize that the size and construction material of the tank will affect your ___weighing___ and ___buoyancy___ under water.

5. Tank sizes run anywhere from 12 cubic feet (340 litres) to 190 cubic feet (5377 litres). The four sizes most common to recreational diving are the aluminum ___65 cu.ft___ , ___80 cu.ft___ , ___100 cu.ft___ , and ___120 cu.ft___ .

6. Two commonly used valves are the ___K___ valve and the ___DIN___ valve.

7. An important component of the tank valve is the ___O-ring___ .

8. A safety feature required of all tanks is the ___burst disk___ .

9. While the tank successfully brings an air environment under water, the ___regulator___ is what allows the diver actually to use that high pressure air.

10. A primary consideration for the diver is how well the regulator ___breathes___ at depth.

11. Regulators have two separate mechanisms: the ___first stage___ and the ___2nd stage___ .

12. The style of ___frist-stage___ that you choose should be based on the type of diving you plan to do, your budget and personal preference.

13. The second-stage works similarly to the first stage, but reduces _intermdiate_ hose pressure to a more breathable _ambient_ level.

14. The diaphragm also functions as a _purge valve_ at the second-stage.

15. In addition to a primary regulator, all scuba units should include a _second air source_ for safety.

16. You should always plan to return to the surface with no less than _500_ tank pressure remaining.

17. The SPG is the diver's _fuel gauge_

18. Knowing your _depth_ is important in adhering to your dive plan.

19. Regardless of your method of putting on the unit, make sure the BC does not interfere with the _weight belt_ which must be free and positioned for easy ditching.

20. Your primary concern in doing the _pre-entry buddy check_ is that you are both ready to enter the water.

21. Unless pressure inside the mask is increased so that it equals increasing outside pressure, the diver will experience an uncomfortable condition called a _squeeze_.

22. If the regulator second-stage comes out of your mouth while under water, remember first to keep _exhaling_ and not to _hold your breth_.

23. Look up and listen for _boats_ while you ascend, making sure your _path is clean_.

24. A skill you'll need to know in case you ever have to make an emergency buoyant ascent, or need additional emergency surface buoyancy is *weight ditching*. If using a belt, first locate it using the _quick draw_ method.

25. After the dive, drain the BC of any water that has entered through the _inflator hose_.

CHAPTER 3 STUDY QUESTIONS

1. The _breathing_ _prosses_ maintains life, and anywhere a person can breathe that person can potentially survive.

2. While lack of training or poor judgement are probably the most common problems, divers who are _overweight_, _smoke_, _drink hevely_, or are generally _out of shape_ may increase their chances of dive-related injury.

3. For diving, it is recommended that the first thing you do is get a _medical checkup_.

4. Anything that restricts breathing, or the flow of air out of the lungs, or the exchange of gases in the respiratory system can make certain divers more susceptible to problems. For this reason divers who have _colds_ or _flu_, have chronic _sinus ailments_ which cause excessive phlegm or blockage of the sinuses or bronchial tubes, or have _asthma_, should seek the counsel of a dive medicine physician.

5. A precaution everyone can take to insure better lung health is not to _smoke_.

6. As with any problem, the solution is to fix the problem, not to react to it emotionally. By consciously returning your _breating_ to normal, and remaining calm and alert, you can avert _stress_ and allow yourself to respond logically.

7. It is a buildup of _carbon dixoid_ rather than a lack of _oxgan_ that stimulates the respiratory center of the brain and creates the urge to inhale.

8. Although oxygen is the gas which sustains life, it only constitutes about _20_ of the air you breathe, while about 80% is _nitrogen_.

9. Remember never to _hold yore breath_; even if the regulator is out of your mouth while under water, keep _exhaling_ a steady stream of bubbles.

10. It is recommended that anyone involved in aquatic activities should be _CPR trained_ .

11. Obvious signs of stress under water are _rabid_ , _shallow breathing_ , and a _wide-eyed_ expression.

12. By ascending too fast you can lose track of your buddy, collide with an unseen obstruction, or worse, risk _over expation injury_ or _de combnson sickness_ .

13. The mask lens in combination with water and the space behind the lens, makes objects appear to be _25_ closer and _33_ larger to the diver.

14. Hearing is affected because sound waves travel about _4_ times faster in water than in air.

15. The most common way divers communicate is by using a number of _hand signals_ devised by the diving community.

16. Anyone who swims knows that when you first jump into the water, even if it's relatively warm water, it feels cold. The reason for this is that the body loses heat faster in water than in air — _25_ times faster.

17. At sea level, atmospheric pressure is about _14.7 psi_ .

18. To _equalize_ ears, pinch the nose shut and blow gently.

19. Any victim of decompression illness may require recompression in a _hyperbaric chamber_ , or "recompression chamber" as it is sometimes called.

20. Being a buddy not only takes competence and caring, it takes _responcibility_ .

21. When you reach the surface, _inclate_ the BC, do a _weight system_ check, keep your _mask_ in place, and either keep the regulator in place or switch to snorkel breathing.

22. After being alerted by the needer, the donor should take control of the situation, offering the most __immediatly__ __availble__   __air__ __sorce__.

23. If the diver becomes aware of being low on air, or has some other __air__ __supply__ problem which has not entirely shut off the air, he or she will be able to swim to the surface.

24. The __emergeny__   __buoyant__   __ascent__ is done in the case of a sudden loss of air which requires an immediate __return__   __to__   __the__   __surface__.

25. Diving injuries and fatalities usually happen because of lack of training, poor judgement, divers exceeding __persnal__ __limaxer__ of skill level or __physica__   __capacity__, or panic; not very often because of equipment failure or environmental conditions.

CHAPTER 4 STUDY QUESTIONS

1. By _planning_ a safe dive and sticking to the plan, problems having to do with nitrogen, such as decompression sickness, can certainly be minimized.

2. As we continue to descend, the total ambient pressure increases, and so do the _partial_ _presure_ of oxygen and nitrogen.

3. Nitrogen narcosis is one of the main reasons it is recommended that recreational divers stay above _100_ _feet_ .

4. If the diver ascends too quickly, the nitrogen comes out of _solution_ and forms _gas_ _bubbles_ in the tissues and blood which can cause blockages and create symptoms of decompression sickness.

5. Just as with overexpansion injuries, the worst form of decompression sickness involves a hit in _the brain_ .

6. Symptoms usually appear within _15_ _min_ to _12_ _hours_ after surfacing, but can appear sooner.

7. Treatment for decompression sickness is immediate _recompression_ in a _hyperbaric chamber_

8. The rate of ascent is _9_ _meters_ per minute.

9. As an extra safety measure, always make a safety stop of _3-5_ _minneuts_ at _15_ _feet_ , regardless of the depth and time of your dive.

10. Recreational divers should never make dives requiring decompression stops, and should also never "_push_" the limits.

11. A repetitive dive is any dive started between _10_ _min_ and _12_ _hours_ after a previous scuba dive.

12. Depth is the _deepest_ point reached during the dive, no matter how briefly you stayed there.

13. Bottom time is the amount of elapsed time from the start of your descent to the time you begin your _direct_ _ascent_ back to the surface.

14. When you begin to use the dive tables, it's easiest to think of them as _three_ _seprate_ _tables_, each with its own function.

15. If you don't find the exact time in the dive table, _round up_ to the next greater time.

16. The group designation letter is used by the diver to figure out how long of a _surface_ _interval_ must be taken before making another dive; that is, how long the diver must stay out of the water before diving again.

17. To keep track of their dives, divers use a _dive profile_. This is a simple graph which includes all the relevant information for recording _no-decomprison_ and _repitave_ dives.

18. There are many things that can interfere with the efficient entrance and exit of nitrogen, including _including age,_ _medication_. (List two)

19. To avoid problems, it is recommended that you wait _12_ hours before flying in a pressurized airplane, and _24_ hours if you plan to fly, or even drive, above 8000 feet or 2400 metres in a non-pressurized aircraft or vehicle.

20. Many dive profiles are actually what we call "_multi-level_" profiles, which means that a diver may actually dive at various depths throughout the dive.

21. Because computers calculate your own personal nitrogen level, divers should not share a _computer_.

> ## *Refer to the SSI Dive Tables on pages 12-13 to complete the following dive problems:*

22. Suppose you make a dive to 51 feet (15.5 metres) for 31 minutes. What is your group designation? __G__. After a surface interval of one hour, what is your new group designation? __F__.

23. Using your new group designation letter from question #22, suppose you want to make a second dive to a depth of 40 feet/12 metres. What is your adjusted no-decompression time limit? __69__ minutes.

24. Using your new group designation letter from question #22, suppose you want to make a second dive to a depth of 40 feet/12 metres. What is your residual nitrogen time? __49__ minutes.

25. Suppose two divers plan a 55-foot- (16.5-metre-) dive for 30 minutes, followed by a 2:15 surface interval. Their second dive of the day is planned to 43 feet (13 metres) for 40 minutes. What is their final group designation? __I__.

DOPPLER NO-DECOMPRESSION LIMITS BASED ON U.S. NAVY DIVE TABLES
SCUBA SCHOOLS INTERNATIONAL SSI®

TABLE 1 — No-Decompression Limits and Repetitive Group Designation Table For No-Decompression Air Dives

HOW TO USE TABLE 1: Find the planned depth of your dive in feet or metres at the far left of Table 1. Read to the right until you find the time (minutes) you plan to spend at that depth. Read down to find the Group Designation letter.

DEPTH feet / metres	Doppler No-Decompression Limits (minutes)	A	B	C	D	E	F	G	H	I	J	K
10 / 3.0		60	120	210	300							
15 / 4.5		35	70	110	160	225	350					
20 / 6.0		25	50	75	100	135	180	240	325			
25 / 7.5	245	20	35	55	75	100	125	160	195	245		
30 / 9.0	205	15	30	45	60	75	95	120	145	170	205	
35 / 10.5	160	5	15	25	40	50	60	80	100	120	140	160
40 / 12.0	130	5	15	25	30	40	50	70	80	100	110	130
50 / 15.0	70		10	15	25	30	40	50	60	70		
60 / 18.0	50		10	15	20	25	30	40	50			
70 / 21.0	40		5	10	15	20	30	35	40			
80 / 24.0	30			5	10	15	20	25	30			
90 / 27.0	25			5	10	12	15	20	25			
100 / 30.0	20			5	7	10	15	20				
110 / 33.0	15				5	10	13	15				
120 / 36.0	10				5	10						
130 / 39.0	5				5							

GROUP DESIGNATION: A B C D E F G H I J K

TABLE 2 — Residual Nitrogen Timetable For Repetitive Air Dives

HOW TO USE TABLE 2:
Enter with the Group Designation letter from Table 1. Follow the arrow down to the corresponding letter on Table 2. To the left of these letters are windows of time. Read to the left until you find the times between which your surface interval falls. Then read down until you find your New Group Designation letter. Dives following surface intervals of more than 12 hours are not repetitive dives.

REPETITIVE GROUP AT THE BEGINNING OF THE SURFACE INTERVAL

	A	B	C	D	E	F	G	H	I	J	K
A	0:10 / 12:00*										
B	3:21 / 12:00*	0:10 / 3:20									
C	4:50 / 12:00*	1:40 / 4:49	0:10 / 1:39								
D	5:49 / 12:00*	2:39 / 5:48	1:10 / 2:38	0:10 / 1:09							
E	6:35 / 12:00*	3:25 / 6:34	1:58 / 3:24	0:55 / 1:57	0:10 / 0:54						
F	7:06 / 12:00*	3:58 / 7:05	2:29 / 3:57	1:30 / 2:28	0:46 / 1:29	0:10 / 0:45					
G	7:36 / 12:00*	4:26 / 7:35	2:59 / 4:25	2:00 / 2:58	1:16 / 1:59	0:41 / 1:15	0:10 / 0:40				
H	8:00 / 12:00*	4:50 / 7:59	3:21 / 4:49	2:24 / 3:20	1:42 / 2:23	1:07 / 1:41	0:37 / 1:06	0:10 / 0:36			
I	8:22 / 12:00*	5:13 / 8:21	3:44 / 5:12	2:45 / 3:43	2:03 / 2:44	1:30 / 2:02	1:00 / 1:29	0:34 / 0:59	0:10 / 0:33		
J	8:51 / 12:00*	5:41 / 8:50	4:03 / 5:40	3:05 / 4:02	2:21 / 3:04	1:48 / 2:20	1:20 / 1:47	0:55 / 1:19	0:32 / 0:54	0:10 / 0:31	
K	8:59 / 12:00*	5:49 / 8:58	4:20 / 5:48	3:22 / 4:19	2:39 / 3:21	2:04 / 2:38	1:36 / 2:03	1:12 / 1:35	0:50 / 1:11	0:29 / 0:49	0:10 / 0:28

NEW GROUP DESIGNATION ► A B C D E F G H I J K

REPETITIVE DIVE DEPTH ▼ ▼RESIDUAL NITROGEN TIMES DISPLAYED ON REVERSE▼

Reorder Nº 2206

DOPPLER NO-DECOMPRESSION LIMITS BASED ON U.S. NAVY DIVE TABLES

SCUBA SCHOOLS INTERNATIONAL **SSI**®

TABLE 3

Residual Nitrogen Times (Minutes)
— CONTINUED FROM REVERSE SIDE —

NEW GROUP DESIGNATION ▶

■ =ADJUSTED NO-DECOMPRESSION TIME LIMITS   N/L=NO LIMIT

REPETITIVE DIVE DEPTH feet	metres	A	B	C	D	E	F	G	H	I	J	K
10	3	39 N/L	88 N/L	159 N/L	279 N/L							
20	6	18 N/L	39 N/L	62 N/L	88 N/L	120 N/L	159 N/L	208 N/L	279 N/L	399 N/L		
30	9	12 N/L	25 N/L	39 N/L	54 N/L	70 N/L	88 N/L	109 N/L	132 N/L	159 N/L	190 N/L	
40	12	7 123	17 113	25 105	37 93	49 81	61 69	73 57	87 43	101 29	116 14	
50	15	6 64	13 57	21 49	29 41	38 32	47 23	56 14	66 4			
60	18	5 45	11 39	17 33	24 26	30 20	36 14	44 6				
70	21	4 36	9 31	15 25	20 20	26 14	31 9	37 3				
80	24	4 26	8 22	13 17	18 12	23 7	28 2					
90	27	3 22	7 18	11 14	16 9	20 5	24 1					
100	30	3 17	7 13	10 10	14 6	18 2						
110	33	3 12	6 9	10 5	13 2							
120	36	3 7	6 4	9 1								
130	39	3 2										

HOW TO USE TABLE 3:
Enter with the New Group Designation letter from Table 2. Next, find the planned depth of your repetitive dive in feet or metres at the far left of Table 3. The box that intersects the Repetitive Dive Depth and the New Group Designation will have two numbers. The top number indicates the Residual Nitrogen Time. The bottom number indicates the maximum Adjusted No-Decompression Time Limit for the next dive.

1

Repetitive Group	ABT	Repetitive Group	Surface Interval	Repetitive Group (For next dive today)
Depth	+ RNT / = TBT: / Bottom Time (TBT)	15 FT. 3 MIN.		

2

Repetitive Group	ABT	Repetitive Group	Surface Interval	Repetitive Group (For next dive today)
Depth	+ RNT / = TBT: / Bottom Time (TBT)	15 FT. 3 MIN.		

WARNING: *The U.S. Navy Dive Tables were designed to Navy specifications for use by Navy Divers. When used by recreational divers, the tables should be used conservatively. Even when used correctly with proper safety procedures,* **decompression sickness may still occur.**

SAFETY STOP PROCEDURE: *It is recommended that you make a 3- to 5-minute safety stop at 15 feet (5 metres) on all dives over 30 feet (9 metres).*

OMITTED DECOMPRESSION PROCEDURE: *Should you exceed the Doppler No-Decompression Time Limits by less than 5 minutes on any dive, it is recommended that you ascend normally to 15 feet (5 metres) and stop for at least 10 minutes or longer if your air supply allows. Should you exceed the Doppler No-Decompression Time Limits by more than 5 minutes but less than 10 minutes on any dive, it is recommended that you stop at 15 feet (5 metres) for at least 20 minutes or longer if your air supply allows.*
Refrain from any further scuba diving activities for at least 24 hours.

    Reorder Nº 2206

CHAPTER 5 STUDY QUESTIONS

1. The surface of this planet is actually made up of very little earth. It is in fact about _72_ percent water.

2. The force that originally acts on the water to create tide is the gravity of the _moon_ and _sun_, primarily the _moon_, pulling at the side of the earth nearest the moon.

3. As tide comes to shore, a _flood current_ follows. As the tide moves outward from shore, an _ebb current_ follows. The period between the currents when no movement occurs is called _slack time_.

4. It is, of course, always a good idea to dive in waters as calm as possible, and concerning tidal currents, this would ideally be during _slack_ time.

5. Because dense, cold water tends to sink underneath warm water, layers of various temperature are found at different depths. The boundaries between these layers are called _thermoclinics_

6. You should keep in mind when freshwater diving that the temperature at the surface may be much warmer than the temperature at your destination depth. Use protective wear according to the temperature you will encounter at that _depth_, not according to what is adequate at the _surface_.

7. By far the most common cause of waves is _wind_.

8. Wavelength is measured from the wave's _crest_ to the _crest_ of the next wave, with the wave _tough_ lying between.

9. Sometimes a relatively stable sea will be disturbed by wave energy coming from conflicting directions, resulting in a sea that essentially moves in two or more different directions. This is known as _confused sea_, and is often the cause of sea sickness.

10. Surf conditions vary widely throughout the world, so there is no absolute method for entry and exit that will cover all conditions. The first time that you dive in this type of environment, or any new diving environment, it is recommended that you dive with a local _SSI Delar_, _Instructor_ or _Dive Con._

11. When choosing a dive site, stay away from _Rocky Shores_ and _never_ _water_ action.

12. _longshore Currents_ flow alongside shoreline and are generated by waves which approach shore at an angle and then are kept from immediately returning oceanward by other incoming waves.

13. Any time waves reach shoreline, that water must return to sea. This returning water creates a back current, or _rip_ _current_.

14. Any time you *do* find yourself facing into a rip current, turn and swim at a _right_ _angle_ or _diangle_ to it until you catch a shoreward water movement, or at least move out of the current's main force.

15. What people think of as _undertow_ is either a rip current or the strong backwash from powerful surf.

16. The greatest variety of life will be visible near the _coral_ _reifs_ in equatorial waters.

17. _corals_ are colonial animals which construct skeletal structures of limestone, often forming extensive _reifs_ in the shallower tropical seas where sunlight and warmer waters prevail.

18. Some corals are brittle and some are capable of inflicting abrasions or cuts. These corals are also easily damaged by _careless_ _drivers_ who kick corals with their fins, or hit the reefs with their tanks.

19. The _fire_ coral is so named because of both its upward plumes of "flame" and because it can inflict a burning sting if you touch it.

20. _kelp_ is not difficult for the trained diver to move through if it is done slowly and carefully, without struggle.

21. The creatures capable of inflicting injury will do so only _defencely_.

22. _els_ are normally quite shy and will avoid confrontation if possible.

23. There is no doubt that some sharks are _unpredictable_, and can be _dangrous_ —but almost exclusively when provoked.

24. Another large fish that doesn't quite deserve its reputation as a hostile predator is the _Barracuda_.

25. Don't be timid about inquiring into the _quality_ and _repution_ of dive expedition businesses and dive boat crews. This is _your_ dive, and again, your comfort leads to your enjoyment.

CHAPTER 6 STUDY QUESTIONS

1. Having a buddy and being a buddy are closely related to another major objective of any dive—being _prepared_ and consequently avoiding _stress_.

2. Most new divers prefer to take their first few dive trips under the guidance of a _professional dive retailor_.

3. Part of dive planning is getting yourself _physically_ ready for the dive.

4. Check all your _equiptment_ ahead of time, and have all necessary repairs done.

5. If you are traveling as a certified diver you will need your _personal credentials_ (SSI certification card and DiveLog), plus it is a good idea to take a current medical history form.

6. Evaluate each other's physical condition. If one of you is _sick_ or very _tired_, it is not a good idea to go ahead with dive plans hoping that there will be an improvement before or during your dive.

7. Be careful to pace yourself, and remember that there is no reason you _must_ dive *every day*.

8. Diving at resorts, with charter groups, or in any vacation situation is fun and exciting, but when you elect to dive, make certain you've taken precautions against becoming _dehydrated_, _exhausted_, or more susceptible to illness, sinus problems or decompression sickness.

9. Drinking _achool_ and keeping _____ hours can lead to dehydration and exhaustion, and can contribute to greater risk of decompression sickness.

10. Be aware of your physical condition and energy level, and put off a repetitive dive if you are at risk for becoming _fatigured_

11. When diving from a charter boat or with any organized group, your diving leader will most likely give a __pre__ – __diving breifing__ about the dive site.

12. When making your own dive plan first, talk about why you're diving, and make sure you are both in agreement about your __objective__.

13. Your __551   Dive log__ provides a convenient check list for site conditions.

14. Discuss a __lost__ or __sepreated__ buddy procedure.

15. Discuss how each of you was trained in __emergency skills__ such as air sharing ascents and emergency ascents because the time to find out is not under water in an emergency.

16. Plan your maximum depth and time and have a __contingency__ plan.

17. As a scuba diver you accept the __responsibiltys__ that accompany certification, but you also gain the freedom to enjoy this wonderful new world.

18. You must understand, however, that just because you are a certified diver does not mean you are __qualified__ to perform every type of diving.

19. The quickest and easiest way to get involved in new diving activities is through __continuing   education__.

20. By keeping track of __weight__ needs in different circumstances, you'll be able to know in advance how much __weight__ you'll require for a particular dive.

21. You'll want to acquire your own __equiptment__ so that it becomes very familiar to you.